MY FIRST ANIMAL
ABC

Silver Dolphin

San Diego, California

Silver Dolphin Books
An imprint of Printers Row Publishing Group
10350 Barnes Canyon Road, Suite 100, San Diego, CA 92121
www.silverdolphinbooks.com

Printers Row Publishing Group is a division of Readerlink Distribution Services, LLC.
Silver Dolphin Books is a registered trademark of Readerlink Distribution Services, LLC.

All notations of errors or omissions should be addressed to Silver Dolphin Books, Editorial Department,
at the above address. All other correspondence (author inquiries, permissions)
concerning the content of this book should be addressed to The Old Dungate Press,
Old Dungate Farm, Plaistow Road, Dunsfold, Surrey, GU8 4PJ, United Kingdom.

Illustration © Maurice Pledger, 2017, courtesy of Bernard Thornton Artists, London.
Written by Amanda Wood
Designed by Jonny Lambert

ISBN 978-1-62686-776-5
Manufactured, printed, and assembled in Shenzhen, China.
21 20 19 18 17 1 2 3 4 5

MAURICE PLEDGER'S ANIMAL WORLD

MY FIRST ANIMAL
ABC

Silver Dolphin

San Diego, California

It's time to play
an alphabet game
to see what animals
you can name.

Turn the pages
from A to Z
to discover this
animal ABC.

A

is for animals.

Armadillo

Aardvark

What animals will you meet?

Anteater

Can you find someone licking up a tasty treat?

Ant

is for beetle and also for …

Bee

Beetle

Bat

B

Bear!

Bee

Butterfly

How many bees has
he found over there?

Bear

C is for lots of curious creatures…

Chameleon

Chipmunk

Including a few with some dangerous features.

D is for dormouse and also for deer.

Dormouse

Deer

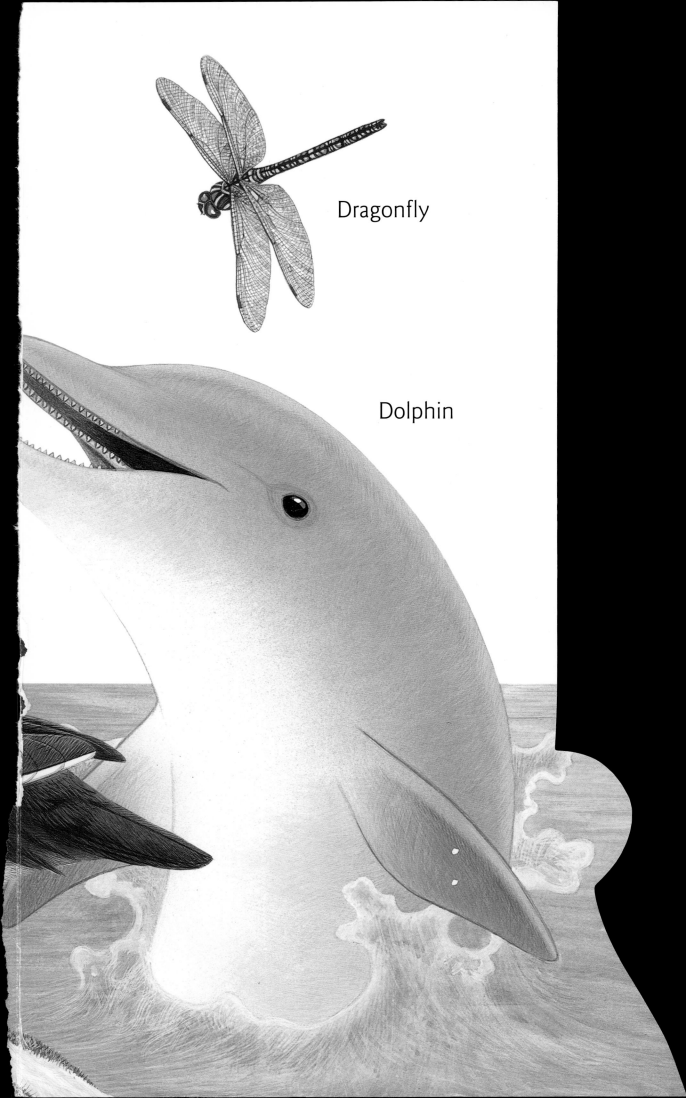

Dragonfly

Dolphin

Who else can you see
who is hiding here?

Cat

Dog

Crocodile

Duck

Caterpillar

Egret

E is for elephant, so big and gray…

Eagle

who's waiting to play.

Emu

And here is her baby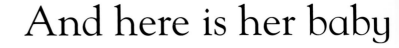

Who else has a name that you've learned to say?

Elephant

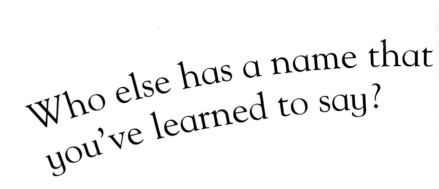

F is for fox, and also for fly.

Who else can you see in our game of I-spy?

Fox

Flamingo

Fish

Frog

G

is for
grasshopper,
jumping
on by.

Giraffe

Grasshopper

Goose

Now can you spot the hummingbird pair?

Hare

Hedgehog

H is for hippo, and also for hare.

Fly

Hummingbird

Hippo

I is for iguana—
a fun word to say.

Jackal

J is for jackal
and also for jay.

Iguana

Ibis

K is for koala,
climbing a tree.
Now open the
flap...

Koala

Kingfisher

Jellyfish

Jaguar

Kangaroo

Kookaburra

Jay

Who else can you see?

L is for lion with eyes shining bright...

Ladybug

Lion

Lizard

Leopard

Lynx

Loris

Lemur

And also for loris, who comes out at night.

Can you count? Come on, let's see. How many ladybugs are in the tree?

M is for lots of marvelous things...

Including this moth with gigantic wings.

Mantis

Monke

Mouse

Macaw

Newt

O

is for otter and
also for owl.

And don't forget ostrich—that curious fowl.

Owl

Opossum

Otter

N is for newt—
who's so very cute!

Moth

Meerkat

Moose

P

is for panda...

Parrot

Panda

the zoo.

Polar bear

Platypus

And polar bear too.

Look for them next time you go to

Ostrich

Penguin

Pelican

Penguin
chick

Q is for quetzal, who has a long tail.

And don't forget that Q is also for quail.

Quetzal

Quail

R

is for rabbit...

Reindeer

Rabbit

Rhinoceros

Now see what the robin
has got in her nest!

Red panda

Can you name
all the rest?

Raccoon

Robin

S is for seagull, spider and snail.

Seal

Snail

Snake

a sea horse
tail?

Sea star

Sea slug

Sea horse

Sea urchin

Now can you spot
with a long, curly

Spider

Sea lion

Seagull

Toucan

Tiger

Toad

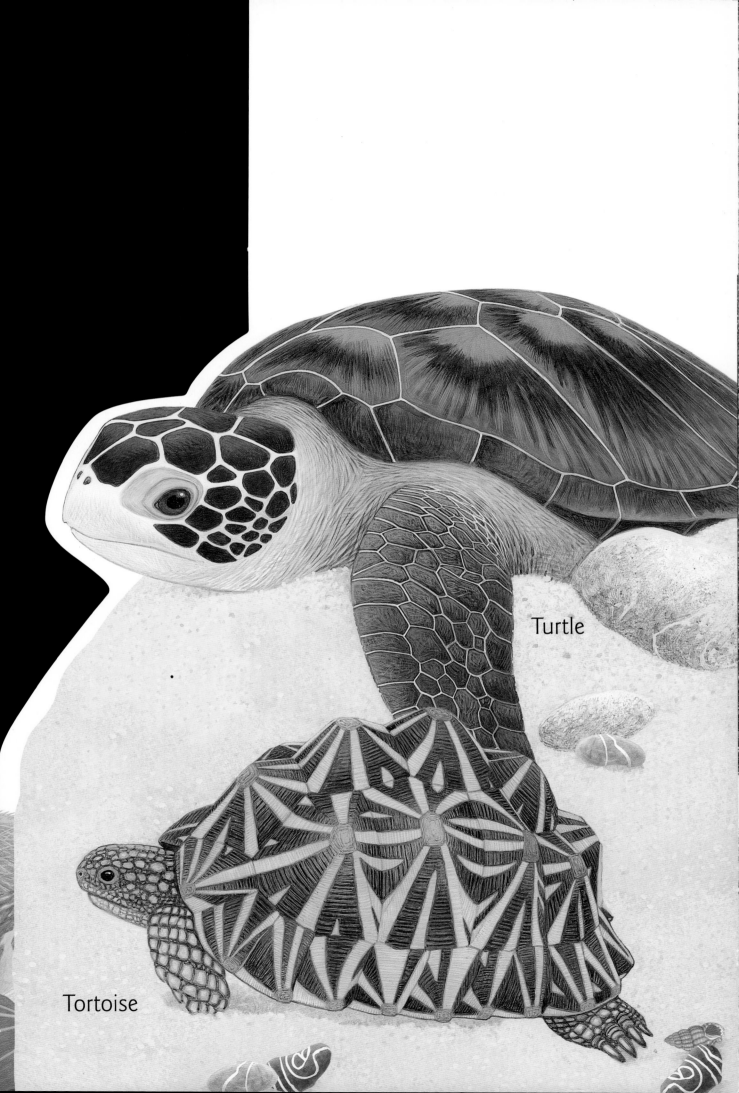

Turtle

Tortoise

Vulture

T

is for toucan, and though it's absurd...

U

Umbrella bird

is for the unusual umbrella bird!

V

is for vole, who lives in a hole.

Vole

W is for whale, large as can be...

Whale

Wolf

Worm

And 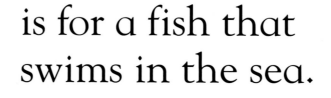 is for a fish that
swims in the sea.

X-ray fish

Now look for a bird
that lives in a tree.
How many more Ws
can you see?

Yellowhammer

Woodpecker

Y is for a great big yak.

Who's that flying over his back?

Yak

Wombat

Z
is for zebra,
at the end
of our book.

Zebra

Now go back to A
for another good look.

Say their names
from A to Z,
and you've learned
your animal ABC!